THIS BOOK IS DEDICATED
WITH FOND MEMORIES
OF MY LATE WIFE

FRANCES

1. Tramway employees are posing in front of the Laird Street Depot sheds on the occasion of the presentation of a gramaphone player to a member of staff. *Rob Jones Collection.*

BIRKENHEAD ELECTRIC TRAMS
1901 - 1937

Charles Rycroft BEM

Design & Origination: Ian Boumphrey - Desk Top Publisher

Printed by: Eaton Press Ltd Westfield Road
                          Wallasey Merseyside L44 7JB

Published by: Ian & Marilyn Boumphrey
                          "The Nook" Acrefield Road
                          Prenton Wirral L42 8LD

ISBN 0-9507255-9-5

Front cover: "Woodside in the late twenties" by GS Cooper.

PRICE
£4.95

CONTENTS:

The Oxton & Claughton Sunday Timetable (right) has been copied from a 1906 Birkenhead Corporation Tramways Official Guide.

Rob Jones Collection.

OXTON & CLAUGHTON CIRCLE.—Via Conway Street.

(Sunday.)

		pm		pm	pm		pm	pm	pm	pm		pm
Woodside	Leave	....	and every 10 minutes to	....	1 30	and every 10 minutes to	1010	1020	1027	1030	and every few minutes to	1127
Laird Street	Pass	1 0		1 40	1 46		1026	1036	1043	1046		1143
Beresford Road	,,	1 8		1 48	1 55		1035	—	1052			
Woodchurch Road	,,	1 13		1 53	2 2		1042		1059			
Charing Cross	,,	1 18		1 58	2 7		1047		11 4			
Woodside	Arrive	1 27		2 7	2 16		1056		1113			

INTRODUCTION:

For forty years the horse-drawn trams had operated on the streets of Birkenhead, offering the residents of Birkenhead an efficient service. However, by the turn of the century they had become old fashioned and obsolete. Electric trams, which had been first introduced into this country in Blackpool in 1885, offered a more efficient, faster and more reliable means of travel. Prior to the turn of the century, Birkenhead Corporation had purchased all the tram tracks in the town and on 4 February 1901, the first electric tram service operated on the New Ferry route.

It was then thought that electric trams were here to stay and they were not likely to be replaced. The first "nail in their coffin" came in July 1919 when a motor bus service began to operate between Rock Ferry and Park Station. Each year saw more and more bus routes being operated and from 1931 tram routes were gradually closed until July 1937 when the final Birkenhead Tramcar operated on the circle route.

This is a history of Birkenhead Electric Trams, based on the personal reminiscences of Charles Rycroft. He began work as a point-boy for Birkenhead Corporation at the age of fourteen and was based at Woodside from 1929 to 1934. After a short period as a conductor on the single-deck route No 79, he transferred to the trams, where he was a conductor on the Circle route until the final day of the Birkenhead Electric Tramways 17 July 1937.

His father John had been a tramcar driver and was interested in anything connected with trams, so it was natural for Charles to follow in his footsteps.

CHAPTER 1.
BIRKENHEAD HORSE-DRAWN TRAMS 1860 to 1901 - A BRIEF HISTORY:

How it all Started:

The street tramway was originated in America in 1832 and was eventually introduced to England by a flamboyant Boston man, George Francis Train, during a short stay in England from 1859 to 1862. Despite substantial opposition from officials in other cities and towns, he was eventually given the go-ahead by the Commissioners of Birkenhead but with several conditions.

All work in connection with the new transport system was to be paid for by Mr Train, he was to keep the roadway alongside the rails in repair and if, after a six months trial, the scheme did not succeed, Mr Train had to remove all the rails and restore the road to its original state.

Within six weeks the rails had been laid on the system, just over a mile in length, between Woodside and Birkenhead Park and the opening date of 30 August 1860 was announced. Mr Train must have realised the significance of the opening of the first public tram system in Europe because he invited all of the many crowned heads of Europe and also the Pope and Gariboldi. They could not have seen the importance of this event, as none of them turned up!

However, the local people were so impressed with the service, comprising two single-deck and two double-deck tramcars, which were each pulled by two horses, that 4,360 passengers were carried on the first day.

A banquet was given for three hundred and fifty guests by Mr Train from 2.00pm at the newly-erected carriage depot, in the yard of Mr Main, in Argyle Street. Mr Main had assembled the carriages which had been shipped over in sections from America.

Mr Train inaugurated a further five tramway systems in this country before returning to America in 1862. There were three short tramways in the centre of London, opening in 1861 and in the following year at Darlington and the Potteries. However, only Birkenhead and the Potteries succeeded, with the London and Darlington ventures being closed by the local authorities because of alleged highway obstruction.

There was some objections to the system in Birkenhead. The omnibus and

1a. Woodside Terminus which opened in 1860, is pictured prior to electrification of the tramway system in 1901. Tram No 16 on the right is standing on the original street railway track. *Ian Boumphrey Collection.*

2. United Tramway & Omnibus Co Ltd tram No 7 is standing at Woodside. This one-horse car is seen full of dockers going to work c1890. *Rob Jones Collection.*

3. Wirral Tramway Company car No 9, built by Starbuck Car & Wagon Co Ltd of Birkenhead in 1880, is standing outside the New Ferry Depot in New Chester Road in the late 1890's.

Ian Boumphrey Collection.

4. This United Tramway & Omnibus Co Ltd horse-drawn tram No 18, is at the Borough Road Terminus. The house behind still stands at the junction with Prenton Road East.

hackney cab drivers were losing business to this new form of transport and some of them would deliberately travel at a slow pace in front of the trams, until they were prosecuted for obstruction. Some of the town centre traders thought they would lose business when potential shoppers would travel by the new trams and improved ferry service to Liverpool. But it was argued that more residents would travel to Birkenhead shops by the new, more comfortable tramcars. Many of the more affluent Birkenhead people complained about the trams passing their homes and the protruding track damaging their carriages. These raised tracks were the main cause for obstruction and the closing of the four services mentioned before.

A Mr Burgess in the surveyor's office, devised a rail with an indent in it and a protruding ridge on the carriage wheels, hence there was no rail visible above road level to cause problems. These rails later replaced the original ones and not only were they popular in Birkenhead, but other towns soon took up the improved track system.

Extensions to the System:

Mr Train, having successfully opened the Birkenhead Street Railway, was anxious to seek pastures new in London and at the end of 1860 he sold his interest to others in the syndicate for £600. This company, styled the Birkenhead Tramways Company, carried on the system for about ten years although they were losing money.

In the summer of 1861 the Oxton extension was built, terminating at the top of Palm Grove, where a new car shed and stables were built (the building is still there today). The line to the docks was laid by the Birkenhead, Hoylake and Deeside Railway Company, who used it as a feeder to the Docks Station. About 1885 the line was taken over by the Birkenhead Tramways Company. The line along Borough Road to North Road was laid c1877 and was extended to Prenton Road East, opening 1 June 1881.

In 1890 there was an amalgamation between the Birkenhead Tramways Company and the various horse bus businesses. The new company, The Birkenhead United Tramway Omnibus and Carriage Company, was granted a ten year lease by Birkenhead Corporation to operate from July 1891 to December 1900.

The Wirral Tramway Company had been set up in 1874 and obtained a Tramway Act authorising it to construct a line between Woodside and New Ferry. However, the line was not officially opened until 1 November 1877.

CHAPTER 2.
BIRKENHEAD ELECTRIC TRAMCARS:

It was in 1899 that Birkenhead Council accepted a tender to supply thirteen single-deck and thirty-one four wheel, double-deck tramcars which were delivered with open-top bodies, as were the trams from an additional order of fifteen, which had the seating capacity increased from fifty-five to seventy-five. All forty-four cars were built by GF Milnes & Co, whose works were originally situated in Birkenhead, at the junction of Cleveland Street and Charles Street. It was the first factory of its kind in Britain.

These tramcars were definitely in the luxury class, having curtains and with the longitudinal seating on the lower deck covered in Wilton carpet which was embossed with the town's crest and bore the inscription "Birkenhead Corporation Tramways" (see picture 5). The interiors were beautifully built, being constructed of English Oak, with the door architraves and lintels over both saloon doors being hand-carved with the town's motto.

The first forty-four were delivered during 1901 and the next eighteen over the following two years. When a further six cars were ordered from Hurst Nelson of Motherwell in 1913, this brought the final tramcar fleet up to sixty-eight cars which consisted of:-

Nos 1 - 13 single deck cars
Nos 14 - 44 open top four wheel double-deck
Nos 45 - 59 open top, twin bogie (eight wheel) double-deck
Nos 60 - 62 works cars
Nos 63 - 68 enclosed top, lowbridge, double deck bogie cars

Tramcar Nos 1-13 were single deck due to the low bridge that spanned Chester Street near its junction with Waterloo Place. Plans were submitted to the Board of Trade to convert them into double deckers, to improve the service on the New Ferry Route. Prior to rebuilding as double deckers, some of these cars were fitted with all round advertisement panels, giving the cars the appearance of open top double deckers (see photo No 6).

The new top deck was to have full length 'knife-board' back-to-back seating which was to be built onto the original clerestory roof with the inside of the seating providing the headroom fore passengers using the lower saloon. Tramcars Nos 1-2 were converted in the joinery shop at Laird Street, the cost being £257/12/10 (£257.64)

5. This interior photograph of the lower saloon on a four-wheeler, was taken at Woodside. The cover for the longitudinal seat was of Wilton Carpet and depicted the Town's Coat-of-Arms.
Ian Boumphrey Collection.

6. No 12 tram is standing at the New Ferry Terminus in New Chester Road c1909.

7. New Ferry Tramcar No 4 is standing at the temporary terminus at the junction of Hornby Street and Chester Street.

8. Tramcar No 8 is standing at Woodside in 1927. The driver's controls can be seen downstairs and upstairs, the longitudinal seating is seen through the door. *Photo Dr HA Whitcombe.*

each and Nos 3-13 were modified by G.C Milnes, Voss & Co at a cost of £200 per tram. The top deck was reached by a short staircase with a 45 degree turn and access to each side of the seating was gained by two doors either side of a short gangway over the canopies. However on Nos 1-2 there was only one doorway, which resulted in fewer seats. All the modifications were completed by 1910. Remotoring of these cars commenced in 1913 but the war put a stop to this and it was 1923 before it was completed. They were remotored with GE 58 4T Motors and also BTH controllers were fitted. In the mid 1920's the controllers were again replaced, this time with BTH B18 controllers. No other modifications were carried out, the service being abandoned in December 1931. The bodies were broken up in 1932, but the frames and bogies were said to have been exported to India.

Tramcars Nos 14-44 were all four wheelers and were delivered with open tops. They were mounted on Peckham 8A cantilever trucks which were powered by two 25hp GE 52 motors and were fitted with BTH B3 controllers. Many cars had their controllers replaced with BTH 510 and between 1923 and 1925 some trams had their trucks replaced by Brill 21E trucks.

One of the reasons that the committee decided in 1903 to fit a top cover was loss of revenue in bad weather. Nos 16 and 17 were chosen for the modification, being fitted with the famous "White " tops (named after the inventor HL White and not the colour). No 17 had the alterations carried out at the Laird Street depot, the cost being £138, with No16 having the work done by Milnes Voss for the same price. Between 1910 and 1913, ten cars were covered in but with the less expensive short covers which were designed by Milnes Voss and then manufactured and fitted by Brush of Loughborough ie. Nos 14-15, 18-23, 38 & 41. A further six were fitted in 1914 by corporation workers at a cost of £119/10/0 (£119.50) ie Nos 37,39,40 & 42-44.

The Board of Trade refused to allow the remaining trams, which operated on the Higher Tranmere route ie Nos 24-36, to have top covers. It is said that a certain councillor who was the cause of the controversy and after he died in the early 1920's, the remaining four wheelers were allowed top covers. By March 1923, Nos 24-26, 34 & 36 had been covered, followed by the others. The design chosen was similar to the "Bellamy" top, as used in Liverpool and Wallasey, with the conversions being carried out at the Laird Street Joinery Shop. The wood used - oak, ash and elm, was supplied by the Parks Committee from trees in Birkenhead Park. All the cars were fitted with six windows to each side and were completed by 1928, at a cost of £150 each. These cars, which were recognised for their distinctive tops with an elliptical shape, were known as the "Tranmere Cars."

Tramcar Nos 45-59 had open tops and were mounted on equal wheel bogies, being delivered during 1902/3. The electric equipment consisted of four 20hp motors and the controllers, which were manufactured in Belgium, were supplied by Witting Bros of London. All cars except No 46 were fitted with "White" top covers, the first being No 52 in 1904. These tops were known for their distinctive ruby glass clerestory windows. Car No 46, which ran on the New Ferry route until the new Hurst-Nelson Trams were delivered in 1913, never saw regular service again.

These heavy bogie trams, which were nicknamed "Dreadnoughts" by their crews, played havoc with the tracks. In 1909, an experiment was made on car No 50, by removing one section of the body and joining both ends up, this shortened the tram by five feet four inches and reduced the weight by six tons. The body was mounted on a Brill 21E truck and received BTH motors. The cost of the modification was £135 and the car rejoined the fleet in 1910, with the seating capacity reduced from 75 to 62. The other bogie cars were to receive the same treatment, but the plans were shelved.

Although the rolling stock was kept in remarkable condition, little or nothing was done over the years to improve the comfort of the travelling public. In 1928, selected cars were chosen to receive a face-lift which cost £200 per tram. Lighting was improved; the old strap bells were replaced with "Numa" air bells; the old familiar gongs were replaced with new ones; sound-proof composition flooring replaced all the old wooden laths on both decks, but the substitute could not stand the wear and tear and wooden lathes were reintroduced. The top and bottom interior decks were stripped of their numerous coats of varnish, revealing the natural oak; the Birds Eye Maple ply on the ceiling was replaced by oak-faced ply; and the "Ever-Dri" seats on top deck were replaced with sprung seating covered in red leather. The longitudinal lower saloon seating was replaced with reversible seats, taking two passengers on one side and one on the other. This proved to be a nightmare for the conductor when there were more than five standing passengers but only nine cars had these seats fitted:- Nos16-18, 40-44

9. These trams awaiting passengers at Woodside prior to 1913, include Nos 15, 22, 58, 29 & 7. Woodside Station is seen to the right, beyond the six-track pole. *Ian Boumphrey Collection.*

10. The driver at the controls of car No 52, which is standing at Woodside, is probably Jack Collister. This was the first Birkenhead Bogie car to be top covered (June 1904). *Photo MJ O'Connor.*

11. Tram No 59, seen on the right at Woodside in 1905. The policeman in the centre foreground, is leaning on the drinking fountain and to the left, in front of the trams is the Point-Boys' box.

Ian Boumphrey Collection.

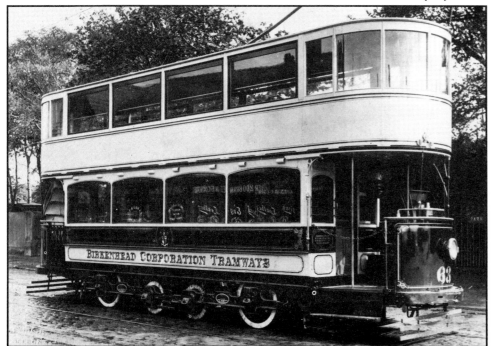

12. Scottish-built car No 63 was one of six specially designed for the New Ferry service. It is seen on the stretch of track from Cavendish Road to the top of Mallaby Street.   *Ian Boumphrey Collection.*

& 50. The others that were refurbished retained the longitudinal seating and were fitted with full length spring cushioning.

Tramcar No 50 had special treatment from the rest, having red uncut moquette seats on the lower deck, brass handrails which were covered in black "Exonite" and it was fitted with a BTH electro magnetic braking system. This was the only improvement for ease of operation over the years. Had a more effective braking system been introduced earlier, Birkenhead would have had a faster tramcar service.

In over thirty years of service Birkenhead had only four trams fitted with driver vestibules, the Department saying that the drivers did not care for enclosed ends. The trouble was that these cars were not fitted with windscreen wipers and in the event of rain, the drivers had to drop their screens to see what was going on! The first to be fitted was No 58 in 1923 followed in 1930 by Nos 36, 42 & 18. The cost per tram was £55.

Tramcar Nos 60-62 were the three works cars, being the 'ghost' trams of the fleet. No 60, which utilised the body of a horse tram, came into service in 1902 as a snow plough. It was also used initially as a salt sprinkler and in 1910 was fitted with carborundem blocks for rail grinding.

No 61 which also came into service in 1902, was a rail grinder and salt carrier and had special facilities to deal swiftly with snow bound tracks.

No 62, like No 60 used the body of a horse tram and was introduced into service in 1902. It became a complete mobile workshop, manned by fully competent staff, capable of coping with any emergency. This car was converted back to a horse tram to celebrate the Borough Jubilee in 1927 (see page 17).

Tramcar Nos 63-68 were built specifically for the New Ferry service by Hurst Nelson of Motherwell and were delivered in 1913. The low bridge in Chester Street meant that the upper saloon had a headroom of only 5ft. 4in. Despite advancement in tramcar design, they did not have protective screens for the driver. These trams were not popular with the platform staff or public as they were unsteady and were so fast that they had notches 10 and 11 of their controllers blanked off. They were eventually retained for peak periods only, being withdrawn from service late 1930, earlier than the older trams.

CHAPTER 3.
BIRKENHEAD TRAM ROUTES:
NEW FERRY ROUTE:

This was the first electric tram service in Birkenhead, opening on 4 February 1901 and using the same route that the horse trams had used. Initially the service terminated at Brandon Street, by the Town Hall, until the track down to Woodside was completed 6 June 1901. The main problem with this route was the low bridge in Chester Street, which carried the LNW/GW Railway to Abbey Road sidings and Cammell Laird's Shipyard. The tramcars ordered for this route, Nos 1-13 were single deck, enabling them to go under this bridge. However, due to the demand on this service, the cars had all been converted to double-deckers by 1910, with reduced headroom on the top deck, allowing for the bridge. The tram service continued until December 1931, when buses, which had operated on the route since August 1930, took over the route completely.

13. Board of Trade officials are inspecting car No 7 on the New Ferry Route 31 January 1901.

14. No 10 tramcar is standing at the New Ferry Terminus with car No 3 in the background. Note the drop windows on the upper deck. *Ian Boumphrey Collection.*

15. Tram No 66 is entering the loop with another about to leave the New Ferry Depot on the right. It was unusual to see two of these New Ferry trams together.

Photo EN Hemmings.

HIGHER TRANMERE ROUTE:

Opening 14 August 1901, the route ran from Woodside to Bebington Road Tranmere, near its junction with Mount Road (see picture 17 - which is one of the only instances that the route prefix " T" is seen on an open-top car). There was the problem of the hill in Argyle Street South, which was too steep for the tramcars. This was overcome by constructing a new s-shaped road linking Argyle Street South with Church Road at the top of Holt Hill (picture 16) and by having tramcars assigned to the route with special brakes worked by a wheel shaped handle below the conventional goose necked brass handle. These can be seen on pictures 16 & 17 - note the cutaway dash at the front to accommodate the extra brake. The new road was named after the then Chairman of the Tramways Committee, Councillor H L Pearson, who incidently was the person opposed to top covers being placed on the tramcars. It has been said that drivers were paid an extra 1/2d per hour on this route, due to the extra skill required in negotiating this hill, but I do not remember them mentioning this. It was decided to widen Bebington Road about 1904 and the buildings on the Mersey side of the road were demolished and the tram poles were moved to the other side, as seen in picture 17. The service closed 29 September 1934.

PEARSON ROAD, HIGHER TRANMERE.

16. Negotiating the steep descent from Pearson Road to Central Station c1904 is car No 25.

Ian Boumphrey Collection.

17. Waiting at the Tranmere Terminus in Bebington Road c1923 is tramcar No 24.

Church Rd Hr Tranmere

18. Tramcar No 29 on the right is passing another tram in Church Road Hr Tranmere 1913.

Ian Boumphrey Collection.

11

CIRCLE ROUTE:

The Laird Street and Shrewsbury Road routes were joined to form the Oxton and Claughton Circle, which opened 2 March 1902. The busy junction of Conway Street and Argyle Street, where the track cross-over had been a traffic hazard for many years (picture No 29), was modified in the latter part of 1928 when American manufactured traffic lights were installed at this junction. These single cluster lights, which were operated by clockwork, were delayed in arrival as they were shipped over in the ill-fated liner the *Ventris*, which foundered in mid-atlantic. The junction of Park Road North and Duke Street (see picture No 20) became a dangerous crossing and also had traffic lights installed later, with the bus and tram stops being set back twelve yards from the junction. Trams were timed to meet at the Kingsmead Road Loop (picture No 21) when both conductors recorded their departure times on the "Bundy" clock. If one car was late, they would meet at the next passing loop either the School Loop or St Aidan's Terrace. This was the last route to close and I was a conductor on the last day - 17 July 1937.

19. This open-top tram is standing in Shrewsbury Road with Gerald Road behind and to the left.
Ian Boumphrey Collection.

20. Woodside bound car No 21 is seen in Park Road North with Ashville Road off to the right, a view taken before the introduction of route letters, in 1913. *Ian Boumphrey Collection.*

21. Car No 32, whose driver was Patsy McDonnell, is in the Kingsmead Road loop, Shrewsbury Road, during the final week of tram operation. *Photo SV Hall.*

LAIRD STREET DEPOT:

22. Tramcar No 19 is entering Mallaby Street from Laird Street. The Laird Street Terminus is beyond the Tramway offices on the right. *Tom Turner Collection.*

LINE of the DOCKS ROUTE:

This route was well patronised by the dock workers, as well as the local population. It was strange therefore that the last car left Woodside at 7.00pm and did not run on a Sunday, yet housing stretched from Argyle Street to Cavendish Street. The route ran from Woodside via Cleveland Street, Beaufort Road and terminated at Wallesey Bridge Road. Although this and the Poulton route, on the Wallasey side of the docks were only half a mile apart, they never linked.

The trams would pass the former GF Milnes in Cleveland Street on the corner of Charles Street, which was the first tramcar factory in the British Isles. The factory closed in 1902 but continued elsewhere until 1905. The similarly named company GC Milnes, Voss & Co (see page 7) was also located in Cleveland Street but nearer to the junction with Duke Street. This factory lasted from 1902 to 1913 and was run by GF Milnes' son, GC Milnes, and the former GF Milnes' chief draghhtsman, Thomas Voss.

23. On the left at Laird Street Depot can be seen tramcar No 18, fitted with a driver's windscreen. This was one of only three cars to be altered this way, in 1931. *Ian Boumphrey Collection.*

24. Board of Trade officials are standing by tramcar No 44 near the Graving Dock in Beaufort Road, on the Line of the Docks Route. *Tom Turner Collection.*

PRENTON ROUTE:

The last horse tram ran along Borough Road 27 September 1901, when the Borough Road depot and stables closed and the new electric tram service commenced. The new system ran along the horse tram route to Prenton Road East, but was extended up Prenton Road West to its new terminus at the junction of Storeton Road. The Borough Road single track was doubled in 1906 after extensive sewer construction work had been completed.

This route transported football supporters to and from Tranmere Rovers. When there was a big game on, the Football Special trams would park the length of Prenton Road West during the match (see picture) which meant that the normal route cars would have to terminate at Woodchurch Lane.

Johnny Pye's bus service from Heswall, which was later taken over by Crosville, was not allowed to travel into Birkenhead and so the passengers had to alight at the bottom of Singleton Avenue and then travel into Birkenhead by Prenton tram. From 1930, Crosville buses were allowed to run through to Woodside.

25. About to depart for Woodside from the Prenton Terminus in Prenton Road W is car No 49.

26. Tramcar No 52 has a broken overhead wire in Borough Road, seen from its junction with Prenton Road West.

Ian Boumphrey Collection.

27. Negotiating the bend from Borough Road, on the left, into Prenton Road West is car No 53.

14

CLAUGHTON ROAD ROUTE:

The horse tramway terminated on this route at the top of Palm Grove where the original tramway offices with a very distinctive lintel over the door stating "Birkenhead Tramway Company" can still be seen today. To the rear was a shed for the horse tramcars and stables for the horses.

When the electric tramway opened on this route 14 August 1901, the terminus was at the top of Park Road East and a horse tramway service was offered to carry the passengers to the top of Palm Grove. After the line was extended to Egerton Road, the horse track in Palm Grove, which was not electrified, was abandoned in November 1901.

The Claughton Road route was a nonentity and the least profitable, so when the manual points at the junction of Conway Street and Claughton Road should have been automated, they were not as the route did not warrant the cost. The centre pole at this junction, seen in picture No 29, had been replaced with side poles and span wires, as seen in picture No 30, taken in 1924. Picture No 30 also shows tram No 35 displaying the CR route letters. In 1925 this was the first route on Merseyside to be abandoned.

28. Tramcar No 44 is undergoing a Board of Trade inspection at the Egerton Road Terminus.

29. Looking down Conway Street from Argyle Street, the tramcar is approaching *The Conway Arms,* in the distance on the left, on the corner of Claughton Road. *Ian Boumphrey Collection.*

30. A similar view to the last picture but in 1924 where the centre pole has been replaced with side poles and span wires. This site was one of the first places in the Borough to have traffic lights.

CHAPTER 4.
BIRKENHEAD TRAM ROUTES
MISSED OPPORTUNITIES:

The electric tram routes were little more than the original horse-drawn tram routes with a few variations and by 1905 the Birkenhead Corporation Tramways system had been completed, with no further additions. With a little more foresight, extensions to the system would have benefitted both corporation and public.

The New Ferry route transported workmen to Cammell Laird one way and girls who were employed at Levers, Port Sunlight, the other. Although the destination board stated Port Sunlight, the service terminated in New Chester Road at the junction with Bebington Road. Bebington Urban District Council would not allow any further extension in their area unless they had full control of the tracks which they would rent out accordingly. This embargo denied Levers' employees living in the Birkenhead and Tranmere areas, a door-to-door tram service.

Many of the outlying districts, with a little more planning, would have enjoyed a tram service for business and pleasure.

The Tranmere route, which terminated at the junction of Church Road and Bebington Road could have been extended to serve Storeton, Barnston, Heswall and other villages in that part of Wirral.

Had the Prenton route been granted an extension to the villages beyond Arrowe Park, this would have eased the town's transport problems when the World Scout Jamboree was held at Arrowe Park in 1929.

The Claughton Road route was, as already stated, a nonentity, terminating at the junction of Egerton Road and Park Road South. Although an extension was sanctioned by the Board of Trade, via Egerton Road, Manor Hill, through Birkenhead Park, Ashville Road, Duke Street and linking with the Line of the Docks route, this was never built.

The Line of the Docks route ran from Woodside via Cleveland Street, Beaufort Road and terminated at Wallasey Bridge Road. This provided an excellent service for dockers and workers at the Oil Terminal but with only half a mile separating it from Wallasey Corporation's Poulton route, it was suggested that the two services should link to run a joint service. However, it took the introduction of bus services by both boroughs to realise the value of a cross docks service.

31. An open-topped tram in Church Road taking nurses on an outing (see opposite page).

Ian Boumphrey Collection.

32. This "Bantams'" tram is waiting at Woodside November 1914 (see opposite page).

Ian Boumphrey Collection.

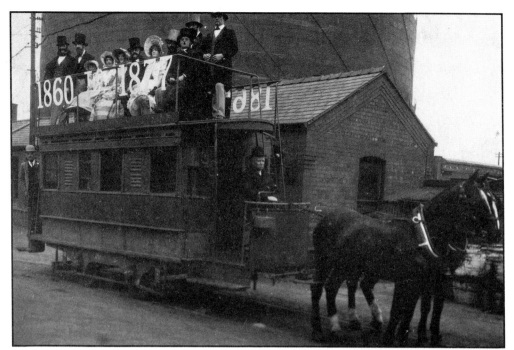

33. This horse-drawn tram at Laird St. depot is celebrating the town's 1927 jubilee (see text).

Ian Boumphrey Collection.

34. This tram was decorated & illuminated to celebrate the town's jubilee in 1927 (see text).

CHAPTER 5.
OTHER TRAM OCCASIONS:

Tramcars could be hired out to the public and the photograph far top left shows an open-top tramcar standing in Church Road, full of hatted ladies. This suggests that it was hired for a nurses outing from St Catherine's Hospital, Tranmere, with the probable venue being Bidston Hill.

The Bantams' Tram:

Soon after the outbreak of the First World War, it was found that many volunteers for the British army were being turned away because they were under the regulation 5ft 3in. Birkenhead MP, Mr Alfred Bigland, took up their cause with Lord Kitchener, who was delighted with Mr Bigland's proposal to form the Bantam division in Lancashire and Cheshire. Recruitment began at Birkenhead Town Hall on 30 November 1914 and the new recruits were taken by tramcar, in batches of sixty, from Woodside to the New Ferry terminus and then on to Mersey Park Schools where they were fed and housed. Mr Bigland, the tall man in a bowler hat, can be seen in the far bottom photograph, standing with the new recruits in front of the tramcar which the corporation loaned for the exercise. The Bantams' motif is seen above the driver.

The 1927 Borough Jubilee Trams:

Two trams were chosen to represent both eras of the public tram system in Birkenhead for the 1927 Birkenhead Borough Jubilee celebrations. Works car No 62, which was formerly a horse car, was returned to that status and can be seen in the top photograph. Members of the platform staff and their wives and daughters dressed up in period costume to depict 1877 and rode on the top deck. Two long standing employees made up the crew, Owen Murphy as the driver at the front and Jack Philpotts, from the New Ferry depot, as the conductor with the grey bowler hat.

The decorated, illuminated electric tram pictured below was car No 27 which was the last of the "Tranmere" cars to receive a top cover and was the only car to have been painted red. It, along with the horse tram, toured most of the tram routes in Birkenhead, being a great success with the public.

1937 Coronation Tram:

One of the ways that Birkenhead celebrated the Coronation of King George the Sixth in May 1937, was by illuminated tramcar. The car chosen was No 22 which had suffered a serious electrical and mechanical fault. However, the relevant work was carried out at the Laird Street depot and the illuminated tram proved to be very popular as it toured the Circle route (see picture opposite).

The Transport Committee decided it should be retained to mark the end of the tram era that July. Slight modifications were carried out to the lighting system, the titles were altered and it ran as Birkenhead's last tram (see page 23).

CHAPTER 6.
A POINT-BOY'S LAMENT:

It was July 1929 at the age of fourteen that I left school. In December I received a card from the local "Juvenile Employment Bureau" requesting me to report to Laird Street Tramway Office the following Monday morning 9.30am sharp!

I arrived on time to be confronted with a number of boys of my own age, dressed in their "Sunday Best" to be interviewed by the General Manager. What an ordeal for us youngsters. Strict discipline was the order of the day and each of us came out of that office wondering just what we had let ourselves in for. I was given the job and after a round of advice and a long list of "do's and don'ts", I was handed my bundle of employee's green tickets and was further instructed by the Traffic Superintendent to report to the Woodside Inspector at 6.00am the following Monday morning.

I duly reported on that memorable cold morning 12 December 1929. By five past six I had manually turned my first Hadfield point, swung on the rope to operate the appropriate overhead "frog" and drunk my first cup of tea from a blue enamelled tea-can. Success at last - ambition achieved - I had joined the long line of point-boys.

Tramway employees rates of pay were by far the best on the Birkenhead side of the Mersey. For example, youngsters leaving school and fortunate to get a post in local government, were paid 7/6d (37.5p) per week whereas

35. Illuminated tramcar No 22 was used to celebrate King George VI Coronation.

36. The point-boy's box to the right of the rear bus is where it all started for me in 1929.

Photo Leyland Motors.

we were fortunate to receive 12/11d (65p) per week and considered ourselves well off. We also received a free uniform every twelve months and a great coat every two years, with free travel when on department business plus fourteen days annual holiday (this did not become the norm for the working class for many years).

Point-Boys Duties

Three boys comprised the point-boys establishment with two boys working an early and late shift and the third on a split duty.

Early shift was 5.55am to 1.00pm with a rest day on Thursday.

Late shift was 4.00pm to 11.45pm with a rest day on Sunday.

The split shift was from 8.00am to 10.00am and 1.00pm to 7.00pm and operated on Monday, Tuesday, Wednesday and Friday. On Thursday the boy on split duty worked from 6.00am to 2.30pm and the boy on late shift started at 2.30pm.

On Saturdays, the early shift was 5.55am to 2.30pm and the late shift from 2.30pm to 11.45pm. The boy on split duty started work at Laird Street garage from 7.30am to 10.00am with breakfast until 10.15 then he accompanied the Chief Cashier with the receipts from the previous day to the bank. He was then free to go home, change, have his lunch and report back for 12.30pm. He was the envy of the other boys as he then finished work at 2.30pm and also enjoyed every Sunday off.

However, when Tranmere Rovers were playing at home, the boy on splits would report to the Inspector on duty at the Fire Station at Whetstone Lane. He would take up position at the points cross-over at the corner off Cook Street and await cars returning from the ground to collect further supporters. Upon the Inspector's signal, the tram was switched over to the outward track. The last football special to leave took the Inspector and point-boy, who together with all the specials crews were given a free ticket to the game .... happy days!

We were fortunate to have a job during the depression and strict discipline was the order of the day, with the passenger always being right. Many a good man was sacked on the spot for a trivial offence.

The boy who worked Sunday commenced at 1.45pm and was on duty until the last tram left Woodside at 11.40pm, ten hours without a proper meal

37. This postcard sent in 1906, shows the point-boy's hut in the foreground and tram No 4 on the right, at Woodside. *Ian Boumphrey Collection.*

38. Football Special cars are lined up in Prenton Road West to transport the supporters after a Tranmere Rovers' game, March 1934. *Photo WE Williams.*

Woodside Terminus:

We point-boys worked under the most exacting conditions, having to brave all weathers. In order to supervise the trams, we operated from the centre of the six-lane track to ensure that each car took its allocated space. The lay-out left a lot to be desired and no doubt two interlaced loops would have solved the problem as all trams leaving Woodside used the same track almost until the points "E" and "F" were reached. Although twenty-two trams could be housed on the six tracks, the variance of the running schedules meant that we had to use our initiative to ensure that certain services got right of way when leaving the grid. To be able to do this, we were expected to memorise the departure time of each route, which changed at the weekend.

Emergencies did occur, which were taken for granted: missing trolley heads, burnt-out controller fingers, broken axles and frayed frog and trolley ropes. Few of the points ever caused trouble as they were serviced regularly by old Jim Warrington, with the exception of the automatic point, the first one on entering the grid. We did not mind this one going wrong as when the inspection cover was removed, small globules of mercury were clustered round the mechanism. We would use a small bottle to collect this precious commodity, which could be used to clean our buttons!

Oh to Drive a Tram!

Every boy has a fantasy to drive a train or a fire engine or pilot an aircraft. Mine was to drive a tram but unfortunately the age for a permit to drive a tram was twenty-five and by the time I had reached this age Birkenhead trams had ceased. However, I mentioned this wish of mine to Hughie MacShane, a driver friend, who arranged to meet me by the Park entrance when he was on the 5.45am duty - the first tram from Laird Street Depot to Woodside. I remember waiting outside George Heron's car showroom opposite the Park entrance and when the tram arrived, I crept round and took up position on the front platform. I was allowed to take over the controls part way down Conway Street and what a thrill it was feeding the current through the controller notches, sounding the gong at intersections, coasting "off current" under the overhead breakers and thoroughly enjoying myself, but Woodside came too quickly. I had many happy unofficial driving trips with Hughie, but my parents would have had a fit if they had known. Poor Hughie was turning the trolley at Laird Street and centralising

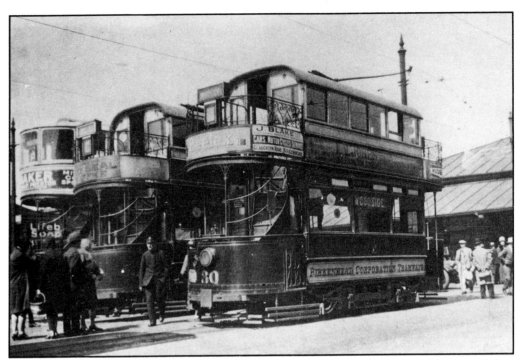

39. Many local business concerns took advantage of advertising on the trams, with some of the firms still operating today.

40. Five of the six grids are occupied by trams, which can be seen in front of the "Ferry To Liverpool" sign at Woodside in 1919. *Ian Boumphrey Collection.*

20

41. Tram No 50 is waiting to enter the grid at Woodside c1925. The cab rank is situated against the hoardings but was later moved to the ferry approach road. *Ian Boumphrey Collection.*

42. The tram pictured centre, No 58, and No 42 on the right were two of only four trams fitted with driver's windscreens (see page 9). *Ian Boumphrey Collection.*

43. Standby trams are pictured at Woodside when during the day at least three cars were kept in reserve to replace any defective rolling stock. *Ian Boumphrey Collection.*

44. Tramcar No 21 is the only tram pictured at Woodside in the latter days of the service and is surrounded by buses. *Ian Boumphrey Collection.*

the trolley wheel to meet the overhead wire, when the trolley wheel sheared the body locking pin. This brought down the trolley head which hit him on the head and he died shortly after. I had lost a good friend.

The Runaway Tramcar:

Birkenhead's only runaway tramcar that I know of, occurred when a driver reported faulty brakes to an Inspector (who happened to be unpopular with everyone) at Woodside. Without any ado the Inspector boarded the tram and took off up the inward track to Woodside and commenced down the ferry approach, feeding the car's motors up as he went. Throwing off current he then commenced manipulation of the handbrake, only finding to his astonishment that it was not working! After going through three sets of points, the twenty-two ton tram had built up a good turn of speed, so he then applied the electric brake. By this time the track and his luck were running out. Due to his incompetent application of the emergency brakes, the tram developed a remarkable "pick up", ran off the end of the track, across the stone setts, mounted the pavement and finally embedded itself into the turnstiles and could have been the first tram across the Mersey! Strange to relate, the imprints of the tram's wheels were still in evidence until the setts were covered over in the late 1940's, over ten years after the trams had finished. The same inspector was involved in another incident when a tram had become "grounded" at Woodside. This was caused by drivers testing their sand hoppers, which left a fine spray of sand deposited onto the rails which after constant use would be compressed into a carbon film. This meant that a tram stopping over this area would not be able to make an earth return to the track. With the use of a point bar jammed between one of the tram wheels and the track, or a bucket of water poured onto the track, the line would usually be cleared. Our inspector noticing a delay and realising the problem fetched a bucket of water and threw it onto the track. However, the driver of the grounded tram had left the controller on one notch and once the water had released the obstruction, the tram lurched forward almost running him over!

45. The successful Tramways football team of 1928-29 left to right: *Bert Bowen, G Minnis, W Beard, Alf Eccles, W Taylor, J Champion, WP Hughes, W Harrop.* seated: *J Bibby, Ted Boswell, Alf Cargill, Bill Cross, Eric Taylor, Joe Brett, Norman Highfield.* Front row: *J Williams, Albert Morton.*

R Fripp Collection.

46. The Birkenhead Corporation Motors and Tramways Silver Band at the Laird Street depot.

Ian Boumphrey Collection.

47. The author at Woodside aged fifteen, dressed in his uniform.

Recreation:

It was not all work and no play as picture No 46 of the Birkenhead Corporation Motors and Tramway's Silver Band proves. It was a generous gesture of the Tramways Committee to allow the formation of a departmental band and to permit the messroom at Laird Street depot to hold their twice weekly practices. Their generosity ended there and the costly outlay for band instruments, uniform and sheet music was met by holding a weekly draw amongst the members of the platform staff. I often wonder what happened to those beautiful instruments which were supplied by Messrs Boosey of London.... no doubt, like the proud bandsmen, they became part of Birkenhead's tramway history.

It is suprising what turns up at a "Flea Market", as picture No 45 proves, which was purchased at Ellesmere Port. It was a glass negative of the successful Thursday League football team in 1928-29, who were winners of the Halligan Cup, the Thursday League Cup and the Melville Cup. Both the Halligan and Melville cups were donated by two active members of the Tramway Committee. The team is pictured opposite in front of a Football Special tram.

The department also boasted a social club and a golfing society. Management and office staff took part in this amenity and if a member of the uniformed staff played the General Manager, woe betide him if he won!

CHAPTER 7.
THE BEGINNING OF THE END:

Events took a turn for the worse in December 1931 when the New Ferry route closed, followed by the Higher Tranmere service, which had declined with the introduction of the King's Road bus service. Also the tram services were cut back to every twelve minutes from Monday to Saturday and were discontinued altogether on Sundays.

This latest cut back meant that we lost one boy and were cut down to two, but Sunday duty had finished, with only two shifts being worked during the week from 6.00am to 2.30pm and 2.30pm to 11.40pm. These shifts continued until 1934 when I was promoted (see page 22), leaving Douglas Newcombe as the last point boy. Then the Higher Tranmere and Prenton routes were replaced by buses, followed in April 1935 when the Line of the Docks route went. The Claughton Road bus service which had replaced the original Claughton Road tram route was extended from Palm Grove to St James' Church, the route being taken via Egerton Road and Tollemache Road. When the Docks route ceased the bus service was extended again via Ilchester Road, meeting up with Beaufort Road. It became known as the North Circle using route numbers 90 & 94. This left the town with only one tram service, the Shrewsbury Road Circular route, which remained unaltered until the final closure on 17 July 1937.

The change over to buses took place overnight and on the following morning Sunday 18 July at 10.00am buses bearing strange route numbers 2 & 6 emerged from the Laird Street Depot. The electric tramcars which had served the people of Birkenhead so well for over thirty years passed into history and a new period had begun.

A Short Break From Trams -Transferred to Buses:

Going back to Easter 1934, when I was in my eighteenth year and having had a pay rise at each birthday, the department realised that I was costing them too much at £1/4/5 per week (£1.21), so they launched me as a conductor onto the Birkenhead public. The single-decker No 79 "shopping bus" was tailor-made for ex point-boys as you had to be twenty-one for double-decker work. Commencing at the Haymarket, the service went up Grange Road to Charing Cross then via Oxton Road, Woodchurch Road as far as the Half Way House, turning right into Storeton Road as far as the terminus at the Arno Gardens. This service was unique as between Market Place South and the top of Oxton Road (with the exception of Charing Cross) there were no recognised stops. Customers would stop outside shops, put out their hands and the bus would stop, likewise passengers wishing to alight would tell the conductor which shop they wished to be dropped off at.

The only problem with my new job was that I was teamed up with Joe, who was well into his sixties and when the Prenton tram route closed, he took advantage of learning to drive buses. He had no qualms when it came to damaging walls in Birch Road and generally keeping the panel beaters busy at Laird Street Depot.

On one occasion we were travelling down Oxton Road at night when Joe pulled up outside a Chemist's shop. After some time I went round to the front of the bus to find out what the hold-up was and Joe informed me he was waiting for the traffic lights to change. Poor Joe thought he was at Charing Cross and the "traffic lights" turned out to be coloured bottles of water in a window display! His one redeeming feature was his dry sense of humour.

I shall always remember the kindness of Mr & Mrs King who owned the general

48. Author on the right aged eighteen having a two-minutes-break at the Arno Bus Terminus in Birch Road, June 1934, with Ernest Pickstock the driver on the left. This bus on route No 79 was a Leyland "Lion" LT2, registration No CM 9389. Note the size of the conductor's enamelled badge - you could almost fry an egg on it!

49. Open top tramcar No 28 in Shrewsbury Road Oxton c1905. *Ian Boumphrey Collection.*

50. New Ferry tramcar No 5 pictured in Shrewsbury Road, opposite St Aiden's Terrace on the Oxton & Claughton route c1915, reason not known.

shop in Birch Road opposite the Arno Gardens terminus. Every morning the first two bus crews would find a pot of tea and home made cake awaiting them. In their memory, a wooden seat was sited at the terminus stop of the old No 79 bus in Storeton Road.

Several conductors asked me if I had seen the manageress of the confectioner's shop at the corner of Storeton Road, but at that time I had not. However, some time later she boarded my bus and before she had stepped off, I knew I was going to spend the rest of my life with her, and being a cheeky eighteen I told her so. She must have believed me as we had over fifty happy years together!

In early 1936, my future father-in-law moved to Birmingham with his family. Frances and I could then only see each other on Sunday, via the GWR 5/6d (27.5p) excursion from Woodside to Snow Hill. It was then that I realised my future did not lie on route No 79, so I had a quiet word in someone's ear in the Time Office at Laird Street and the following Monday morning I commenced conducting on the trams, at the higher wage of £2/17/0 (£2•72)

It is interesting to note that the No 79 bus pictured opposite, CM9389 - departmental No 128, was re-painted in the original livery of scotch purple and cream, although bus No185 (which was the last petrol-engined bus to be delivered) had already been delivered in the new colours of light blue and cream! Bus No128 was wrecked following a German air raid 12/13 March 1941.

Back Working with Trams Again:

There was a wonderful camaraderie that existed between the various tram crews with cakes or sweets being shared out at tea breaks. What fun it was working with them and as there were a number of "comedians" we had plenty of laughs.

One thing that did grieve me was the apparent lack of maintenance that the trams had suffered in such a short period. This was particularly noticeable when going through a loop in the track and whilst standing on the rear platform you could see the whole of the staircase separate from the platform structure only to re-join when regaining the straight track once again.

Local Characters:

We had a few amusing characters among the residents of Oxton and Claughton. One I distinctly remember was a retired Cavalry Major from the 1914-18 war. He would take up a pose on the open front balcony of the tramcar complete with sword in the shape of his walking stick, his scabbard being a cigarette packet.

He would wait for the tram coming through the loop from the opposite direction and he would engage the tram in full cavalry style. This was quite harmless until he broke a few windows, but it did break the monotony!

We also had some charming passengers and I recall the Spanish Ambassador and his wife who resided in the Beresford Road area. Alas they must have been "royalists" because they disappeared overnight when Franco came to power.

Another gracious lady was Miss Dempster, daughter of the shipping magnate. She wore decorative hats which were liberally festooned with flowers or imitation fruit. She would board the tram and after wishing her "good day", she would often look at you very hard and ask if you had been off work because she had not seen you for a long time. You might reply in the positive and were rewarded with 2/- (10p) to treat yourself with. You could possibly pick her up on the return journey and the same conversation would repeat itself - how could you argue with a lady with such a pleasant outlook on life?

Another personality was a gentleman we christened the "tannerman" who would board the tramcar in Shrewsbury Road at the junction of Colombia Road, always sporting a brown stetson type hat and smoking a Churchillian cigar. On boarding the tram he would give you 8d (3.5p), this was 2d (1p) for his "workman's return" and 6d (2.5p) -otherwise known as a tanner- for yourself. This could purchase a packet of ten Capstan cigarettes and would be a daily gift worth in excess of 50p today!

CHAPTER 8.
THE LAST DAY:

The 17 July 1937 was a sad day for many Birkenhead people, not only was it the end for many tram drivers who were too old to change to driving buses, although they were offered driving instruction, but it was the end of an era which had started back in 1860, with Europe's first public tramway system. I recall at 11.55pm on that sad night standing with my parents at our front door in Borough Road, about two hundred yards from Whetstone Lane. Then we heard the long familiar hum of the car's motors and Borough Road took on a strange glow. A moment later, around the slight bend from Central Station came illuminated tram No 22 which looked like some wonderful

51. Charles Rycroft pictured at the controls of tramcar No 23 at the Kingsmead Road loop in Shrewsbury Road, Oxton, on 16 July 1937, the day before the Birkenhead Tramway system was abandoned.   *Tom Turner Collection.*

52. Illuminated tramcar No 22 is pictured here as the last official Birkenhead tram that ran on that sad day 17 July 1937.

Tom Turner Collection.

transformation from fairyland (the Transport Committee had decided to have an Illuminated Tramcar for the Coronation festivities of that year and had retained it for this final role).

The driver chosen for this last tramcar service was an old friend, Owen Murphy, who was the department's oldest driver, whose service went back to the old horse-drawn tramcars of the last century. As the car drew abreast of us Owen "threw off power" and gave us a significant wave, then picking up speed once again it disappeared around the corner and into history.

We returned sadly to our home, my dad and I looking at one another not daring to speak, knowing how pent up we were. It must have been a very sad day for my father, as he was a definite "Tramoholic" who would patiently answer all my questions regarding the Birkenhead Fleet. He ate slept and talked trams, so it was the perfect association we had, discussing for hours the whys and wherefores of each individual car and he even carried a DIY Tramway Manual for Peckham Trucks. It was a useful item to have containing such hints as: "how to replace or by-pass a faulty control finger", "how to replace motor brushes" and a host of "getting back to the depot unaided" hints.

My father never had a day's illness from driving a tram and facing the elements without any protection and yet when he took up bus driving, his health declined and whilst I was still in the army he passed away in March 1945. I shall miss his companionship and I suppose I shall mourn him until I too pass on.

Strange to relate that from that eventful night in 1937 right up to the day he died he never mentioned trams again.

APPENDIX 1.
THE ROUTES AND FARE STRUCTURE:

All routes converged on Woodside Ferry approach, as here was the main link with Liverpool, via the Mersey Ferry and by rail from Hamilton Square Station, which was two minutes walk away. Birkenhead's rail link with the rest of the country was also here at Woodside.

Public Opening Dates for Routes:

New ferry: (To Brandon Street) - 4 February 1901
             (To Woodside) - 6 June   1901

Higher Tranmere:	- 14 August	1901
Claughton Road:	- 14 August	1901
Laird Street:	- 14 August	1901
Prenton:	- 27 September	1901
Line of Docks:	- 24 December	1901
Circle:	- 2 March	1902

Tram crews, with one or two exceptions, rarely exchanged routes during their working day and although the fare structure was fool-proof, by modern standards it was positively archaic. The ruling was one route, one ticket box complete with pre-printed tickets apertaining to that route and the waybill was similarly pre-printed with stages to be completed in the spaces provided en route. If, for instance, a crew was asked to work a football special, the conductor when clocking on would receive two ticket boxes, one for his normal duty and the other would be a "Prenton" ticket box. Believe me, one ticket box was heavy enough! Another confusing fact was that tram stages did not overlap and a conductor who normally worked on the buses found the complex list of fares beyond his comprehension. Having to contend with an overhead trolley in addition to this meant he would be thankful to return to his bus conducting duties. The bus

53. Above: This is a model of Woodside Ferry Approach which took the author six years to construct and is correct in every detail, even the adverts have been scaled down to size and are in their true colours. The remarkable tram models were built by Tom Turner. *Photo by Tom Turner.*

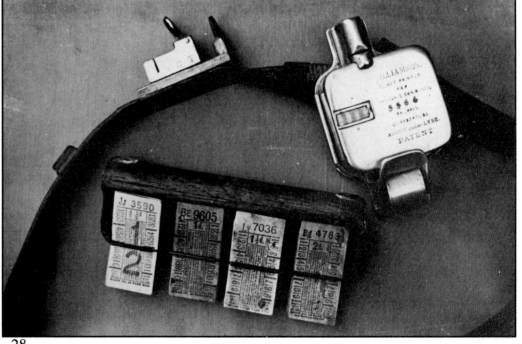

54. Picture right: The ticket holder complete with original Birkenhead tram tickets is seen below the leather strap which holds the ticket cancellation clipper, used to cancel the workman's and bus and boat returns. The Williamson ticket punch on the right dates back to Birkenhead trams and when they were scrapped, were then used on the buses until the early 1950's, when automatic ticket machines were introduced. *Tom Turner collection.*

Birkenhead Corporation Tramways.

HINTS TO PASSENGERS.

The Tramways Committee beg to offer the following few hints, in the hope that they will contribute to the comfort of Passengers and to the efficiency and usefulness of the department in general.

Wait until the Car stops.

Allow passengers to alight before boarding Car.

Enter or leave the Car quickly.

Have your Fare ready, and remember it is difficult for the Conductor to change large coins.

Keep your Ticket until you alight.

When all seats are occupied kindly move to the front of the Car.

Consider the convenience of fellow-passengers in the matter of seating accommodation, ventilation, &c.

Smokers are requested to take the rear seats on the Tops of Cars, and non-smokers the front seats.

It is dangerous to lean over the sides or through windows of top decks of Cars.

Passengers are not allowed to stand on the tops of Cars.

Tramway Stopping Stations are signified by tramway poles being painted white. One red ring—Cars Stop on request; two red rings—All Cars Stop.

Property found on Cars is taken to the Woodside Tramway Cash Office, where application for same should be made.

Passengers are requested to give timely warning to the Conductors of the Station at which they wish to alight.

The Corporation reserve the right to alter or amend the Time Tables herein as found necessary or desirable

Economize and energize.—By making good use of Tramways you save time, shoe leather and energy.

The above "Hints to Passengers" was copied from a 1906 Birkenhead Corporation Tramways Official Guide.

Rob Jones Collection.

fare lists were compiled on a graduated scale but the tram fare list was printed as follows:-

1d Stages.
1. Woodside to Duke Street.
2. Argyle Street to Laird Street.
3. Park Entrance to Upton Road.
4. Duke Street to Howbeck Road.
5. Laird Street to Beresford Road.
6. Upton Road to Palm Hill.
7. Howbeck Road to Balls Road East.
8. Beresford Road to Fire Station.
9. Balls Road East to Conway Street.
10. Wilmer Road to Woodside.

1 1/2d Stages.
1. Woodside to Laird Street.
2. Argyle Street to Upton Road.
3. Duke Street to Beresford Road.
4. Laird Street to Balls Road East.
5. Palm Hill to Argyle Street (Conway Street).

2d Stages.
1. Woodside to Beresford Road.
2. Park Entrance to Fire Station.
3. Upton Road to Woodside.

Please note that this fare and stage lay-out is from memory only.

The graduated fare lists adopted for bus operation was by far the more simple yet efficient of the two systems eg. On a bus leaving Duke Street outwards from Woodside, the conductor would punch all his tickets in stage number 4. Whereas his counterpart on the tram would punch his 1d tickets in stage No 4, his 1 1/2d in stage No 3 and his 2d in stage No 2. All very confusing - but it worked!

Workmen's Fares

Workmen's Returns were issued on all tram routes leaving Woodside before 7.30am and covered the full journey. The returns were issued for day-of-issue only and were suitably printed to eliminate misuse on the corresponding day of the following week. There were only two prices - 1d single or 2d return.

Bus and Boat Returns

The 5d return was issued from the Park Entrance to Woodside (inward from Laird Street) or from the Fire Station via Central station to Woodside.

The 6d return was issued either way on the Circle route from Howbeck Road to Woodside. The return could be made on the day following that of issue.

Children's Fares

Children accompanied by a fare-paying adult travelled free up to the age of three and above three years of age they travelled at half the price of an adult.

Miscellaneous Information
re
Birkenhead Corporation Tramways.

Length of Single Track... ...	23'53 miles.
Total Number of Cars	59
Number of Cars with Top Deck Covers	16
Seating Capacity of Cars, Single Deck	33
Single Truck Double Deck ...	55
Double Truck Double Deck ...	75
Passengers carried per annum	11,052,114
Receipts per annum	£53,341
Wages paid per annum... ...	£17,616
Number of employees engaged	230
Number of miles run per annum	1,319,079

DATES OF OPENING OF ROUTES.

New Ferry...	Feb. 4th/01
Higher Tranmere	Aug. 14th/01
Claughton Road	Aug. 14th/01
Conway Street to Laird Street*	Aug. 14th/01
Shrewsbury Rd. to Beresford Rd*	Sept. 27th/01
Borough Road	Sept. 27th/01
Line of Docks	Dec. 24th/01

*Formed into Circle, March 2nd/02.

PLACES OF INTEREST
in and around Birkenhead to be reached by Tramway :—

PLACE.	ROUTE.	FARE from Wdside
Drill Hall	Claughton Road Car to Slatey Road and 1 min. walk..........	1½d.
Music Hall......	Claughton Road Car to Entrance	1d.
Olympian Gardns Adeler & Sutton's Pierrots	New Ferry Car to Bedford Road and 3 minutes' walk..........	1d.
Argyle Theatre and New Theatre Royal	All Down Cars going to Woodside (except New Ferry Route) pass doors. N. Ferry Route—Alight at Market Street.........	—
Birkenhead Park	Claughton Road or Circle via Conway Street Car to Park Entrance..........	1d.
Mersey Park....	Higher Tranmere Car to Downham Road and 1 minute walk	1½d.
Victoria Park....	Higher Tranmere Car to Park Entrance	1½d.
Arno Park and Oxton Village ..	Circle Car to Gerald Road and 5 minutes' walk, or Borough Road Car to Terminus and 10 mins. walk...................	2d.
Bidston Hill and Flaybrick Hill Cemetery	Circle Car to Upton Road and 5 minutes' walk....	2d.
	Or Dock Car to Terminus and 10 minutes' walk..	1½d.
St Mary's Church Abbey, and Old Priory	New Ferry Car to Abbey Street and one minute walk............	1d.
Pt Sunlight Vill'ge	New Ferry Car to Terminus and 5 minutes' walk....	2d.

The *Miscellaneous Information and Places of Interest,* listed above, were copied from a 1906 Birkenhead Corporation Tramways Official Guide.

Rob Jones Collection.

56. The number 18 open top tramcar, which is Woodside bound, is passing in front of the Birkenhead Higher Elementary Technical School c1906. The centre poles seen here were later replaced with side poles and span wires. *Ian Boumphrey Collection.*

55. This is a different view of the horse-drawn tramcar pictured on page 17 and is seen at the Laird Street Depot. It is helping to celebrate the Birkenhead Borough's Jubilee in 1927. Members of the platform staff are seen with their wives and daughters, dressed up in period costume to depict 1877. The tram used was works car No 62, which was formerly a horse car and had been returned to that status for the celebrations. *Ian Boumphrey Collection.*

57. Tramcar No 29, which has the letter "T" above the Borthwick's sign and signifies it operated on the Tranmere route, is passing in front of the famous Argyle Theatre in Argyle Street. *Ian Boumphrey Collection.*

APPENDIX 3.
TRAM RESTORATION:

When the trams finished in the town, many of the bodies were sold off to make caravans, chicken coops etc. A local haulier purchased the body of car No 20 and had it transported to Farndon, where for about forty years it served as an auxiliary bedroom to a bungalow on the banks of the River Dee. The tram was found in 1977 and although one side had faced the weather for forty years and was in poor condition, the rest had survived remarkably well. It was not moved from this site until 1983 when it was uplifted and transported to Speke for restoration by members of the Merseyside Tramway Preservation Society. A Brill type truck was found in Barcelona and shipped over.

The partly restored Tram No 20 took part in the 1988 Port Sunlight Centenary celebrations. There were many misty eyes when No 20 put in an appearance and one elderly passer-by said to me "Remember these?" and I was able to proudly retort, "I not only remember them, I actually worked on them!"

What a sight No 20 will be with the original livery of maroon and cream, authentic numbering and lettering together with the hand-painted original Birkenhead Coat-of-Arms faithfully transposed on each side by Tom Turner-this being just one of many thousands of jobs that have been hand-done by helpers over the past ten years.

The Tram Museum is presently being built by Wirral Borough Council at Woodside - I never thought that I would see the day when a Birkenhead Tram ran at Woodside again!

58. Body of car No 20 being removed from its home of forty years on the banks of the River Dee at Farndon in 1983. *Photo by J Annison.*

59. The restored Birkenhead Tram No 20 being transported to Port Sunlight to help celebrate the village's centenary. *Photo by Glynn Parry.*

ACKNOWLEDGEMENTS

I would like to take this opportunity to say a special thank you to my friend, Tom Turner, who provided me with the costing details which had hitherto been a closed book to me. Thanks to him also for making his Birkenhead Memorabilia available. I am grateful to the Merseyside Tramway Preservation Society and to The Friends of Birkenhead 20 for their assistance. Also to Glynn Parry for his help copying the photographs and to my friends, of whom there are too many to mention, who lent the photographs, which I trust makes this publication worthwhile.

ABOUT THE AUTHOR:

Charles Rycroft was born in Wilton Street, close to the Birkenhead Park entrance, in 1915. His was a close family, his father worked as a driver on the trams, his mother looking after Charles and his sister, Louise, at home. Growing up in a close-knit community and being sent on errands, he can still remember all the local shops, the names of the shopkeepers and the price of the goods they sold. He left school in July 1929, aged fourteen, at a time when there was a recession and jobs were hard to come by. Although Charles was keen on electronics and had constructed a crystal wireless set at the age of nine, it was against his parents advice that he joined the Birkenhead Corporation Tramways, as one of three point-boys, in December 1929.

At Easter 1934 he transferred to buses as a conductor on the No 79 "Shopping Bus" which he says were the happiest working days of his life. It was on the No 79 bus that he met his future wife, Frances, who was at the time the manageress of Barnes Confectioners Shop in Woodchurch Road.

In 1936 she moved with her family down to Birmingham and as Charles had decided there was no future on route 79, this move spurred him on to have a quiet word at Laird Street depot which resulted in him being transferred to trams as a conductor on the Circle route. He continued in this position until the trams finished on 17 July 1937 and then transferred to the buses as a conductor on the same route.

He was married to Frances in 1939 and later that year, after war was declared, joined the forces where he was twice mentioned in despatches and was awarded the BEM for special services. After the war he returned to working on the buses from 1946 until 1953.

Following a succession of jobs he moved to Hawarden in 1965 and finally retired there in 1980. He then spent six years building a scale model of Woodside Ferry Approach and also writing his memoirs.

60. The author is pictured at the controls of the restored tram No 20, when it was on display at Woodside in July 1992 for the "Tall Ships" event. *Photo by Glynn Parry.*